Praise for *Disease of Kings*

"Anders Carlson-Wee's Midwest is not the Midwest of Bly or Wright, with their farms and coal towns, but a contemporary portrait set in late capitalism. There are dumpsters to dive behind the Whole Foods; Cannondale bikes to steal on campus. The young men in this book seem to struggle to craft selves, hatching plan after plan to get a little more, do a little better, maintain the freedom they've bought, borrowed, or stolen. At the heart of *Disease of Kings* is male friendship, which toggles between intimate and distant, tender and tough. As Carlson-Wee writes, 'Isn't that the secret indulgence / of friendship: being near what you / can never be?'"                                    —Maggie Smith, author of *Goldenrod*

"Anders Carlson-Wee travels in and out of utter-noir midnight to lightening-dawn hues with such aplomb, his poems seem effortless. Yet his rigor of focus crosses borders of every kind. He manages a virtuoso's dance through the book's many astonishments, making elegance feel easy, which it is not. Expect acclaim."
        —Luis Alberto Urrea, author of *The House of Broken Angels*

"[An] extended parable of friendship. . . . [R]esonates with the heart of humanity. *Disease of Kings* reveals our deepest secrets and failings with complex sympathy."
                        —Dustin Pickering, *Los Angeles Review*

"Groundbreaking."            —Alexis Sears, *Diode Poetry Journal*

"Carlson-Wee writes exquisitely about loneliness. . . . *Disease of Kings* is both a thoughtful meditation on the cost of going it alone and an emotionally devastating treatise on the need for human touch and connection."  —*Rain Taxi Review of Books*

"*Disease of Kings* showcases a mastery of tone and voice, an uncanny ability to talk to you (reader) like a friend and confidant, while telling you the hardest truths—truths that might actually change your life, truths the world doesn't necessarily want you to know. These poems are urgent without being demanding, confessional without being sensational, and indirectly lead us to reconsider the nuances of relationships, how our lives are structured, and ultimately the big questions of what matters most."
—Joy Baglio, *Common*

"[*Disease of Kings*] tell[s] the stories of . . . a world touched by deprivations and suffering . . . but also by beauty and plenty and joy."
—*Rumpus*

"Questioning statements rake each page with an athletic sureness that, to its major credit, never succumbs to the . . . sentimental."
—*Harvard Review*

"Carlson-Wee's skill and versatility [allow] narratives and meditations and monologues and . . . lyrics [to] intermingle, not as they do in a sculpted narrative but as they do in a consciousness. The poems are by turns candid, self-justifying, lonely, angry, cocky, embarrassed and, distinguished from embarrassed, ashamed. (I'm not sure I've ever seen an ordinary, unromantic sense of shame so well rendered.) . . . The overwhelming emotion of the book . . . is marrow-echoing loneliness, and here Carlson-Wee's ability to meld intensity and understatement shines."

—Susan Blackwell Ramsey, *32 Poems*

"These slices of life feel real. These poems went down smooth. They left me wanting more." —*Heavy Feather Review*

"[*Disease of Kings* has] a real-world, practical elegance [that] resonates with its own kind of music" —*Dante's Old South Radio,* NPR

"[Carlson-Wee's] poems read easily, propelling the reader through the book with a steady voice whose music is swift and consistent."

—*Body*

"I love Carlson-Wee's ability to handle complex subject matter with a clarity of language and form that [allows] the third-dimensionality of this book to shine through. . . . Carlson-Wee is able to carry a speaker's voice with such precision."

—*Washington Review of Books*

"[*Disease of Kings*] is loaded with . . . fascinating characters. . . . [An] impressive collection of poetry with its sustaining message of faith and hope in the human spirit."

—Jack Grady, *Diode Poetry Journal*

"[*Disease of Kings*] is so cohesively solid."

—Taylor Brorby, *North American Review*

"Poems full of freedom and gratitude, rejoicing even in lack, and providing us with another vision of how to live successfully."

—Rachel Custer, *Open: Journal of Arts & Letters*

"*Disease of Kings* is nothing short of a *coup de maître*."

—*Preposition*

"The searching [in *Disease of Kings*] is more spiritual than physical, the restlessness more intimate than expansive. In the narrative that drives much of the collection, the speaker and his friend North scrabble to live off the fat of the land, which in the 21st century U.S. means taking advantage of the endless waste of a consumer economy. They dumpster dive for food and raise cash by holding fake moving sales with items they've scavenged. Other characters—odd, sad, sometimes generous—pop up in the poems, their fleeting presence a kind of counterpoint to the deep relationship with North. The speaker, ultimately left on his own, remains adrift in solitude he can neither give up nor settle into comfortably: 'The longer I'm alone / the smaller a gesture could be // and still console / or rattle me. Strange to need // so little, but to need it / so badly.'"

—Maria Browning, *Chapter 16*

Disease of Kings

ALSO BY ANDERS CARLSON-WEE

*The Low Passions*

*Dynamite*

# Disease of Kings

poems

ANDERS CARLSON-WEE

**W. W. NORTON & COMPANY**

*Independent Publishers Since 1923*

All rights reserved
Printed in the United States of America
First published as a Norton paperback 2025

For information about permission to reproduce selections from
this book, write to Permissions, W. W. Norton & Company, Inc.,
500 Fifth Avenue, New York, NY 10110

For information about special discounts for bulk
purchases, please contact W. W. Norton Special Sales at
specialsales@wwnorton.com or 800-233-4830

Manufacturing by Versa Press
Book design by Chris Welch
Production manager: Lauren Abbate

Library of Congress Control Number: 2024948032

ISBN 978-1-324-10511-4 pbk.

W. W. Norton & Company, Inc.,
500 Fifth Avenue, New York, N.Y. 10110
www.wwnorton.com

W. W. Norton & Company Ltd.,
15 Carlisle Street, London W1D 3BS

1 2 3 4 5 6 7 8 9 0

*In memory of my grandfather*

*Roald Carlson*

# CONTENTS

# II

# III

# IV

# V

Disease of Kings

The love I've known is the love of
two people staring

not at each other, but in the same direction.

—FRANK BIDART

# Hired

The Grand Am's window rolled down
but it was too dark out to see in:
a hand waved me over, a voice asked
if I wanted to make some quick cash
standing right where I was standing
for the next ten minutes, simple as that.
Just stand here? I said. Simple as that,
the voice said, and the hand stretched out
a twenty. It was weirdly humiliating,
doing what I was already doing.
Like being told to act natural on camera
and sensing that who you are is failing
to entertain. Ten minutes passed.
Fifteen. Twenty. I'd never made so much
in such little time, never been so nervous
doing nothing. I kept needing
the car to come back, some sign
it was over: a horn, a gunshot, the rising
pitch of oncoming sirens. I could accept
I'd never know what I'd been used for,
but I wanted proof it was finished.

# Cora

The rats want what we have. They come at night and scratch in the kitchen, the pantry, looking for a way in. Most nights they only get at the bin below the sink. Leave them alone, North says, but I keep jamming steel wool into cracks. Our place is saggy plywood shelves, couches found on corners, tables made from crates and pallets—whatever we can't push in our sales. We're not actually moving, but we throw a moving sale every couple months. Fuck a yard sale. A moving sale makes people hungry.

Next month I come home with a cat. North sees how it is and gives me the silent treatment, but he loves Cora. Come here, Cora. Cora girl, my pretty Cora. I teach her how to hunt with a feather teaser. She gets so good she breaks it. When North gets into bed and curls on his side, she climbs up the covers along his body's ridgeline, purrs down at him from her perch on his shoulder. North puts a bell on her collar so the rats can hear her coming. I take it off. We throw our next moving sale and almost everything goes. Doesn't matter, North says, as if the sale was something that happened to us. We'll find more. A lady rolls down her window: Didn't you boys move to Texas two months ago? North keeps putting the bell on Cora. I keep taking it off.

A week later we're sleeping on camping pads because our beds both sold. Shrieks wake us. We rush to the living room and flick the switch. Still as the Sphinx, Cora sits where a couch used to, watching half a rat crawl away from itself. The back half lies limp in front of her, tail pinned beneath her paw. By small turns of her neck, she clocks the awful progress of what is still alive, innards painting a wet streak across hardwood. But before the moving half can reach the darkness it desires, Cora pads over and launches it back to the center of the bare floor. Leave it, North says when I get my knife and start forward. It's natural. All this is natural.

# Listening to North in the Morning

I know it's a frittata because last night
we dumpstered a boatload of eggs
and I can hear the tap tap tapping
on the lip of a bowl. I count the cracks
and smile at eighteen because he's breaking
the record. Shuffle of socks on the floor.
A suction gives way to a low whir
and I know he's in the fridge. Butter
and cheese for sure, but what else
is he rummaging for? Five trips
to the counter before the door sucks shut.
Chopping. Scraping. More chopping.
The sizzle of the pan reaches me
before the scent of garlic does.
I like listening to him get reckless,
even though half of everything is mine
and I'd never waste so much on one
meal. Isn't that the secret indulgence
of friendship: being near what you
can never be? Now the unoiled
backdoor and he's out in the garden.
Rosemary. Wild onion. He's talking
to someone, but who? His laughter
is strong this early in the morning.
Now back in the kitchen making a hard

patter of something: Did he find
that Colombian dark roast I hid
in the bottom drawer? I hope he did.

# Footprint

Throw away eggs and I make
breakfast, plastic and I weave

rugs, duct tape and I reinforce
a chair leg, milk cartons

and I plant seeds, start
a nursery. Your torn jacket

gets hemmed. Busted shades
get jimmy-rigged. Throw away

Tidy Cat buckets and I add
hardware, convert them to rain-

proof panniers. Your mail
and I read it. Your pencils

and I write. Throw away
hundreds of pounds of tea

and I draw baths thickened
with hundreds of bags

of chamomile. Bent nails
straighten. Warped wood warps

back. Throw away frmes
and I frame whatever else

you threw away, hang it
on my wall like a portrait.

# Where I'm From

Grinning and flicking me off,
Gavin left practice and climbed
in the car beside his mom
just as my ex-girlfriend's new
boyfriend was drunk and doing
90 past the high school.
A small-town constellation.
Seatbelts would have done
nothing, authorities told us.
As if that blunted something.
Amber gave birth just before
the sentencing. The new father
did time in juvie, in time
was set free. At the double
funeral my father preached,
Good Shepherd Lutheran
so full they had to roll a TV
into the nursery for overflow.
Toddlers stacked blocks, zoomed
Hot Wheels. The janitor got
confounded by a cluster of cords—
picture came through, but no
audio. In black and white
I watched my father climb
into the pulpit and silently
say what no one could believe.

# Snow

It was the law: you had four hours
after snowfall to get your sidewalk cleared.
Our landlord hated the chore so much
he paid us five bucks per inch toward rent.
North shoveled, I came behind
with salt that glowed in the streetlights
like a second snow, as if we were unmaking
and remaking the conditions. That winter
North's dad disappeared again, but this time
North didn't bother to report it.
Thanksgiving passed. Christmas came
and went. It's deep but it's easy,
North said one night, tossing load
after load over his shoulder, the powder
twisting in the sky and shushing
against his coat. Each time the snow let up
we pored over weather reports, hoping
for blizzards. If it keeps up like this,
I said, February will be free. In March
his dad was back in town, twenty pounds
lighter with no explanation, fishing
for little loans. When he heard about February's
good fortune he started leaning on North.
My own dad had never asked me
for anything and I wondered what

it would mean to know him that way.
The snow kept coming down.
What are you gonna do? I said, fanning
cupfuls of salt on the concrete.
North shrugged: Give him February.
You can't, I said. North lifted a shovelful
and heaved it. Stop picturing your own dad,
he said. By April, February was spent.
In May North asked if his dad could move in.
He was much younger in person
than North had made him seem.
We gave him a closet, but soon his shit
was everywhere. This is temporary,
I kept saying. Without snow
the rent outdid us. I caved and made the call,
my dad covered most of the summer,
treated the three of us to dinner.
I'd forgotten how embarrassing it was
when he offered to pray over meals,
but glancing around the table I realized
everyone was grateful but me.

# Ambition

To suffer none of it.
Money, work, or obligation.

To face the days free
of roles. No title. No position.

To get by on found food,
castoff clothes, scams
and hustles and handouts.

To wonder about judgment
less than about stealing
the time it takes to wonder.

To have stolen time. And be lost
on how best to squander it.

# Call and Response

I try him on a whim and all I get
is voicemail. Ben, I say when I answer
my cell a week later. But it's not Ben.
It's his sister telling me he's in
the hospital for no one knows
how long. I've had this conversation
before: one by one my old friends found
dead, or faded on pills in Fargo,
or inpatient and slowly going. It's become
who's next and how long do we have?
I go back to the kitchen where
North is busy making us enchiladas.
Who was that? I don't answer. I watch him
wash tomatoes. He's so gentle
with them, I have to look away.

# I Feel Sorry For Aliens

Lonely nights I walk to the old
elevator that used to hold Montana

grain: beams rusted, train tracks
ripped out, a patchwork of missing

roof panels framing perfect squares
of starlight: an ambition pursued

for 80 years and 80 years only.
I think of aliens puzzled by this

failure long after we're gone.
How fickle the human will seem.

How slapdash. How make-do.
And as they tour the world's ruins

who'd blame them for assuming
we lived our lives alongside other

species of us? How else to forgive
the dissonance between

the vision that built Venice,
the vision that built Butte?

# Moving Sale

Duluth, we said when a browser asked.
Omaha, we said to another.

Omaha? they said. What's in Omaha?
It was a good question, but in truth

we weren't moving, just using
the drama to draw shoppers.

How much is this lamp? said a lady
in yoga pants. Everything's labeled,

North told her. Another lie:
we left labels off the expensive shit,

buying us time to spot the weakness
in each person. Sold, I said

when she opened way too high.
Brainerd, Mankato, Des Moines:

whatever sounded likely in my mind.
Between customers North cracked

jokes, had me going, but my secret
was that if I'd been alone I would have died

of shame. I recounted the money.
Get it? he said. Get it? trying to break

my concentration. And the sale
went on like that: Where to?

What's in St. Louis? What's this cost?
Why would you want to live there?

Honolulu, I said, testing
somewhere better, farther away.

A year later when I actually moved
it was less than a mile.

II

# Lou

You don't start at zero. You start way below zero.
You got your gas money, admission, you grab
a dog and a beer and hit the ATM, which takes
a not-so-small fee. By the time you set eyes
on horses you're down thirty, forty bucks
and you haven't even placed a bet. I started coming
when my wife died. She wouldn't marry
a gambler, so after her funeral was my first chance
in 47 years. Oh, I don't bet a lot of money.
If you don't bet a lot you can't make a lot,
but you can stay in it. Some guys hit the Pick 3
and the Superfecta—those guys are gods. Not me.
I just work the chalk and try to climb outta the red.
To tide me over, my wife used to let me bet
chocolate chips. We'd watch the races on TV
and place our bets in bowls. She'd tease me
for playing it safe. Loosen up! she'd say,
then she'd put it all on Here Is Happy to win.
She loved that horse. She'd lose, of course,
and go make cookies with her losses
while I worked the chalk. After 47 years of that
it's hard to remember I'm betting real money,
losing real money. When I win I remember,
I can tell you that much. I'll never be a god
but I'm still here. The only god I ever met in person

was my wife. No bullshit: she hit the Superfecta
one time. Filled her bowl on four horses
and named the order. The exact order:
1, 2, 3, 4. And she won. After we stopped shouting
and cussing and jumping up and down
we did a little two-step right there on the living
room rug, and at the end I even dipped her.
She had red hair for miles. It was beautiful.

# B&B

Before North took a seasonal job
fishing for kings in Alaska
I'd never admitted to myself
that he was my only friend.
For a little income and to cope
with the lonely summer, I rented out
his room at a nightly rate, listing it
online as a bed and breakfast
so I could charge more. I hid
all his stuff in the closet, took photos,
and at the top of the post I wrote
*eco-friendly*, but never explained
what that meant. Evenings
I'd check-in tenants, then leave
on my rounds to various
dumpsters, keeping ahead
of the week's trash pickup schedule.
Back home, I'd wash
the food I'd found and count
our stocks—staying above a hundred meals
was important to me. Over bacon
and blueberry pancakes
my first tenant told me it was only
after his wife died that he could finally
pursue his lifelong passion

for gambling. Catnapping
on a Monday afternoon, I missed
another call from my mom,
who was retiring soon and wanted
me to hear her preach
one last time. She was good
at justifying my lifestyle, calling it
stewardship of the Earth,
the saving of small parts of God's
creation. As if she didn't know
how cheap I was, how greedily
I clung to each free hour
of each free day. Running
the B&B was the most work I'd done
in years, and that was nothing
but living how I always did
plus keeping the lights low
so the sheets looked clean.
July brought windless days, air so thick
you could feel yourself passing
through it. Unprecedented highs,
the weatherman said, sweeping
his arms apart as if to make room
for the heat. All the dumpsters
became ovens, spoiling

the food and plummeting
our stocks below sixty. Whoa,
one tenant said during a Pepsi commercial,
I forgot how beautiful what's-her-face is.
Even after I started skipping
a meal a day, the stocks
kept dropping, so I simplified
the B&B's breakfast menu.
I knew I'd lose stars online,
but with North coming back at the end
of summer it wasn't like I was trying
to build a presence. The end
of the world already happened,
another tenant told me
as I made her a PB&J. Now
the most important thing is to avoid
contact with trees. Think about it,
she said. We mustn't touch them.
Both of us had sweat rings
in the pits of our shirts, and as we spoke
they spread. I cut off her crusts
and served her sandwich on a blue plate.
She tapped the windowpane:
Watch for unnatural colors
in the sky—that's the mood ring

God's wearing. Each week,
another historical record
was broken. If tomorrow
is like today, the weatherman said,
I'll see you folks at the beach.
Online, a tenant gave me one star
because I didn't have A/C.
Another, because I had a cat
and hadn't said so. In August
a salmonella scare fed the dumpsters
and shot our stocks into the black.
Upon arrival, my guests found
complimentary Clif Bars
on their pillows. My stars went up.
I ran out of Ziplocs.
I could have gone back
to three square meals, but I froze
the bulk of it, wanting to impress
North when he got home.
Sometimes I heard footsteps
in his bedroom and let
myself pretend it was him.
On her final day in the pulpit
I took the 17 to see my mom preach.
After the service, members

of the congregation kept touching
my shoulder—I'd been dragged
to enough funerals to recognize
the gesture. My mom
looked tired, her eyes sad
but also full. She hugged everyone.
She knelt down and hugged
the children, her bright vestment
enwrapping all but their tufts
of hair. There was no question
about what mattered or if
she loved me. I excused myself
to the bathroom and cried. In the end,
August shattered all previous Augusts.
I stopped looking at my stars.
My final tenant talked
about a series of inventions
he claimed to have come up with
that would all but put to shame
our current way of life.
Patents are pending,
he explained over coffee and toast.
Now it's only a matter of time.

# Spirits

We'd lift gin from your mother's cabinet
and walk the hallways of Robert Asp Middle
taking swigs in plain sight from a 20oz
Pepsi Clear, your gap tooth flashing
at teachers we passed, your hands forgetting
to pass the bottle, screwing and unscrewing
the cap. After that I moved. We lost track.
The news was six months old by the time
I heard. When they don't say what happened
you know what happened. We used to catch
rides from highschoolers out to the Red to jump
the bridge. Water thick with clay. Red with clay.
We kept close watch for underwater logs.
Smoked Menthols. A 40-foot drop into swirls
of currents. One time you stayed under
and kicked downstream to trick me. Nervous,
I stared at the surface for signs. No signs.
I stumbled down the bank to dive in.
The moment you were certain you had me
the valley cracked with your laughter.

# Cups

Hovering near the line I watch a lady
order coffee and ask for a second,
empty cup. But once she has the cup
in hand she thinks better of it
and, leaving, drops it in the trash.
I know about cups. They're trees
ground to a pulp and coated with thin
skins of plastic not unlike condoms
that make recycling impossible.
In ninth grade I kept a Subway cup
in my locker and cradled it
each day at lunch beneath my coat
as I trudged through subzero winds
and gusting snows to the franchise,
where I'd blend in with the crowd
who'd already ordered, then step
boldly toward the soda fountain
patrolled by the staff and fill my cup
with Sprite, Dr. Pepper, Mello Yello,
Cherry Coke, making what we called
a graveyard. I had the cup so long
I named him. Bathed him daily
at the drinking fountain near the gym
and never let his lip get torn

or pinched. What stopped all this
was Subway updating its logo—
instantly my cup looked old and wrong
and I couldn't keep making my graveyard
unless I was willing to switch
to a new cup, which I was, and did.

# Another Thrill

Half the night trying to think
of the right word for the thrill
of finding the most expensive
shampoo you can buy and all
the next month punishing
dandruff and built-up grease
until your hair shines and falls
in little golden locks and then
walking into the shop
for the first time in your life
to return the empty bottle for
cold cash no questions asked.

# Barb

Oh trust me, honey, you don't wanna know
about the pelvis of a doe I found
in a Johnny Rockets, or the bone broth
made from stray dogs, or the raccoon burgers.
That's whiskey talk, if ever. Don't worry—
I won't inspect your kitchen, I don't work
B&Bs. Besides, am I running late!
How long did you say to the airport? No,
don't tempt me: egg whites will do me fine.
And bacon. And a pancake, but cut me off
at one, and no butter. Just so we're clear,
all that blood and guts and gore—that's extreme
cases. After all, it's scheduled mostly:
they know I'm coming and I know they hide
what they don't want me to find. Good riddance.
You think I wanna see that kind of junk?
It's a wink-wink occupation, this line.
Like cops parked out on roads inhaling donuts
and just because they're there the traffic slows.
That's basically my job. Intimidation.
Where'd you find this bacon? You're kidding.
It's not at all the way you'd think it would be.
I've got a record, that's why. Nonviolent.
It was a job I could get and get quick.
Pays fine. What I like is the power trip:

seeing fear in men's eyes, bosses pretending
not to be bosses to buy themselves time,
saying yes ma'am, yes ma'am, yes ma'am, terrified
I'm gonna find mouse poo on my walk-through.
To own a man like that without as much
as opening your trap—God I'd be rich
if I could bottle it. Please say there's more
of this bacon. Bless you. I'll wolf these strips
and zip. I grew up most everywhere.
I left home young but should've left younger.
Never had a plan, never wanted kids
so never needed Mr. Right. I like movies
alone and martinis together, my cat's
name is Boots and I don't do drama—
that about covers it. Which of these clocks
is right? Can I smoke in here? Fuck it.
You know that butter you mentioned? Get it.
I guess I close about ten joints a year.
The human factor is the biggest bitch.
Cut finger, that kind of thing. If your bleach
is off one part per million, cute, happy
to let it slide. But if that puddle of blood
didn't leak from a piece of veal . . . Last year,
if you can believe it, I found myself
working my own favorite joint, a surprise

inspection. Caught a big infraction, too.
Between us, they didn't need to bribe me.
I could've found a lot more than a tooth
and still been keen to keep them clean—
you don't just stumble into manicotti
that good. Okay, okay, another pancake.
Is that rosemary I'm tasting? You sneak!
If it wouldn't mean completely missing
my flight, I'd take your kitchen by force
and sniff out what your little secret is.

# Trash

Kneeling in a mix of good and bad
I sort by smell, never noticing
the garbage truck's approach,

not hearing, over the trainyard's
lonely horn, the scrape of forks
sliding into the dumpster's black

sleeves, until the machine
is lifting me like an offering
into the thick midsummer air.

Seconds later, after getting chewed
out by the driver, threatened
with arrest, and left behind

with the now hollow dumpster,
I can't help but wonder what
would have happened to me if

I'd been taken away with the trash.
No doubt added to other masses
of trash, swept west by train car

and dumped on a bulk barge
bound for some poor other place
where they stuff the world's mecca

of waste, only to have some kid
not so different from me find
and dream up a use for my belt.

# Where I'm At

I'm alone, sipping water in a café,
when the barista says, Excuse me,

sorry, someone asked me
to give you this, and hands over

a fifty-dollar gift card.
There must be a mistake,

I say out of shame. But I know
it's for me. It's like Aladdin's,

the thrift store where I hunted
deals for months before realizing

Moonflower, the owner,
was making up discounts

out of pity, because I was looking
so hard. Or the time a stranger

found me sifting through a Walmart
dumpster, newborn baby

strapped to her chest, snowflakes
catching in his wispy

black hairs, and passed me
a wad of twenties, saying,

I've been where you're at. No,
I wanted to say. You're the one

with a baby. But as quickly
as she came, she cupped

the newborn's head and stepped
across an ice patch

toward her car, and I said
the only thing there is to say.

# Oscar

Fuck no she didn't leave me over money.
She left me cause I have no ass. It's true—
a belt holds on my hips about as good
as an oiled-up pole dancer. That's why
I invented these strapless suspenders.
Can't see em, can you? Good, that's the idea.
Almost went bankrupt makin the prototype.
My wife kept sayin, What suspenders?—
you aint wearin nothin. But riddle me this:
Are my jeans pooled at my feet? I swear,
bonafide genius dumbfounds belief
with simplicity. Same goes for the truth.
Like if I told you my wife left me cause
I got less milkshake than a garter snake,
you'd say there's gotta be more to that story.
Like what? I go to work one day and come
back home to no trace of her. No photos.
No toothbrush. Not even the carrots
she raised in the garden beds, just holes
in the earth like buckshot where she plucked em
free. And of course, she got custody.
And the house eventually, which, I'll admit,
I mortgaged to pay for the patent.
You think that was the dagger? Here I am
workin to cure auto-pantsin for the assless

and she's fussin over a little loan? Yes or no:
could I win her back if I doubled down
and got those silicone implants? Fine,
shake your head, but I don't think you respect
how bad it is when God forgets to blow up
your balloons. Hell, I'd show you, but these
suspenders are a bitch to get back into.

# House Fear

Not wanting to waste energy or pay
for energy wasted, but also hating
the idea of being afraid when I got back,
I stood with my hand on the switch
for a long time, suffering over the light.
Coming home two nights later I saw
dark windows and couldn't remember
what I'd chosen. Soon I was certain
something was wrong—the bulb
could be bad, but didn't I just change it?
The power could be out, but it's on
at the neighbor's. I tested the door:
it was locked but only by the bolt—
was I that reckless? Stepping inside
I swore the air smelled different.
Hello? I said. And then desperate
to prove I was alone: Hello! Hello!

# III

# Sea Change

Fresh back from Alaska
North can't stop talking about it:
the scale of the ships, the mountains,
the hauls of kings brought up
in a hundred and fifty fathoms
of net. You're not picking up nickels,
he says. You're locking down a buck
every time you touch a fish.
His stories leave me sheepish
about our humdrum routine:
circling the store to make sure
closing crew's gone, then dropping
into hills of black plastic bags
we sort by weight. North foxtails
the heavies toward me, I rip in and fish
for what's good: grape juice,
squash, hotdogs dusted with floor
sweepings we'll have to singe off.
All summer, he rode the open sea,
hoisted ropes hand over hand,
pounded meals of raw salmon. Now
he's built like a Greek statue:
sleeves rolled, forearms popping veins,
and each time he flexes to lift a bag

he looks godlike, unbreakable.
Dude, he says, I bet we could
sell this shit, start a business.
Profits. Employees. A marketing
approach. How far his mind goes
I'm afraid to imagine.
I sniff to see if the chicken in my hands
is bad. It is. Who would buy this?
Anyone. People like us.
I wipe cold grease on my pants.
But we wouldn't buy this.
North shrugs, drops a rotten plantain
and reaches for a persimmon.

# Caught

You ran to draw
the cops away, convince them
you'd acted alone.

But once you got
beyond a Maglite's reach
they found me

half-hidden behind
the plywood and 2-bys
we'd been stealing.

That pissed them off.
Who's your buddy?
they demanded, turning

me and tightening
the cuffs. I had to
give them something:

a name, an age, a color
of hair. It was easy
to make it believable.

What caught me
off guard was the pleasure
I took in changing you.

# Andrew

We each get food stamps in two states. I'm Iowa and Minnesota. North is Michigan and Minnesota. I have the same name in both states, but for some reason, in Michigan, North is Andrew. Covering my ass, he says. Wiping the paper trail clean. No one's after your ass, I say. Exactly, he says. They're after Andrew's ass.

Before we sell them, we browse Whole Foods for stuff you never find in dumpsters. North grins at me by the caviar. Can you believe this? he says. Us? Shopping? At the checkout counter he enters the wrong pin for the wrong state, has to run the card twice. Back outside I say, Why'd you give the cards different pins? North looks at me like I'm crazy. Because they belong to different people, he says.

We walk past the 19 and Nicollet Diner and on toward the Convention Center, looking for a buyer. I hope Andrew doesn't get busted, North says. I smile, trying to think of how to lengthen the joke. They're not after Andrew: he only has food stamps in Michigan. That's true, North says, Andrew's probably safe, but here's the thing: I'm Andrew. I know you're Andrew. No, I mean my real name, it's not North, it's Andrew. I stop walking. I turn to face him. You're kidding, I say. Andrew shakes his head.

# Gout

During the attack I was happy
to take care of North. Each morning
I'd heat water, wrap his foot
in blankets, and dole out painkillers
I dumpstered from Walgreens
and kept hidden in an empty jar
of laxatives. The disease of kings,
Wikipedia called it, caused by
overindulgence, excessive amounts
of red meat. No more bacon,
I told him. No more steaks.
But each time I came home the kitchen
reeked of grease. Don't look at me
like that, he said. It was November.
No snow yet. In the afternoons
I went down to the banks
of the Mississippi where I'd recently found
a castoff fiberglass boat. To make it mine
I'd dragged it up a dry creek
and covered it with leaves.
The benches were missing,
transom was rotted out, but the work
wasn't beyond me. Without knowing
why, I decided to keep it
from North. I could hear him coming

no matter where I happened to be:
each one-legged hop on his powerful
frame made the house quake.
Cutlery rattled in its drawer
like loose change. The shakers
drifted slowly apart on the table.
Where? he said. Fucking tell me.
I told him he'd get his next Oxy
when he stopped eating crap.
The problem was how easy it was
to find rich foods. And not just some.
Ungodly amounts. We ate a diet
we never could have enjoyed
if we'd been paying for it. Mornings
I kept an eye on his intake,
but when I left for the river
he gorged. Keep it up, I said,
and you're gonna lose that foot.
His birthday was only days away
and as I worked on the boat I tried
to think of what to get him. Not cake.
Nothing food related. A black V of geese
flew low overhead, following
the river's course. Voices carried down
from foot trails, impossible

to parse out. I fixed the transom.
I put in particleboard for a bench.
Our life as it was, North wasn't
getting better, hadn't left
the house in weeks. One night
when I checked, the painkillers
were missing. I didn't say anything,
but after he went to bed early,
against all my natural impulses
I emptied the kitchen. The chest freezer's
bottom layers were so iced in
I hacked them out with a hammer.
I heaved it all into the neighbor's trash.
The next day, when I opened
the fridge, each item was back
in its place. I checked the cabinets,
the freezer—all was restored.
North was passed out on Percocet.
I fumed. I debated. I changed
my mind and let him sleep. Before dawn
on his birthday, I put on a mask
and got a wheelchair from emergency
at St. Mary's. No one chased me.
I packed a bag, wrapped his foot,
and wheeled him to the river,

his bad foot propped on his good
for elevation. Faster! he said
as I steered him around imaginary
dangers. To make the last hundred feet
he used my body like a crutch,
hobbled downhill through the trees.
When I unveiled the boat, he didn't
ruin it with words. He knew me.
Drifting midcurrent with the leaves
gone, we could see everything.
Squirrels. Piles of trash. Plastic bags
resting in eddies. The tarps and tents
of the homeless. Joggers on trails,
the small cloud of each breath.
On the far shore, so many cardinals
had gathered in one tree
it appeared to be fruiting.
It took us all day to float to St. Paul.

# The Juggler

When he tells you his name he stutters.
When he haggles over the price

of your food stamps he stutters. When he claims
his dad forbade him to star in the play

and that's what led to the boredom and coke
and that's what led to the first car

he stole he stutters. It's there when
he says where he sleeps. When he tugs

on a blunt and doesn't talk at all
it's still there. But when he unzips

his bag on the busy corner and unpacks
the gas and torches, belting out a call

to draw the already gathering crowd,
almost screaming over the tired moan

of rush hour traffic, promising fire
and knives and hula-hoops and magic,

his voice comes out clear. Smooth.
Travels to the passing ears like wheels

greased and loaded with the elusive
weight of words. Perfect Rs. Perfect Ts.

As if we could sing what we can't say.
Catch what we can never hold. Now

the ring of the crowd tightens for the show.
Collectively hushes as the necks

tilt back and the first blazing torch
spins into the sky's dark throat.

# End of Term

Down on one knee, North hacksaws while I stand lookout, a thick glitter of metal shavings on his arm. Tomorrow, all the bikes left on campus will be impounded. Orange tags hang from crossbars like so many prayer flags, signed and dated by the chief of campus police. This one's mine, North says. Whatever, I say. He raises the seat for me and I ride it the short distance home while he shops racks for expensive brands.

By the time I jog back he's found the next three: a Giant and two Cannondales. Forget that last one, he says, this baby's mine. Fine, I say, but no more switches. Back from my eighth ride home, campus police rolls up on me to ask if I've seen anyone suspicious. Suspicious how? The fatter officer leans out the window: Like they don't belong on campus. I look around us at the empty street. How can you tell who belongs here?

When I find North he's booking it through a parking lot wheeling bikes on either side of him. No limp. No sign we couldn't have been swapping jobs. So much for his gout. They're onto us, he says. He hands off the Surly and in the same motion mounts the Bianchi. This one's my real one, my Black Stallion. I don't even look at him. He knows what he's doing but he's doing it anyway.

# Blizzard

I wake so full of silence
I know it snowed all night.
Make coffee, toast. Scratch
tic-tac-toe in the windowpane's
frost and beat myself.
Coat, hat, gloves, boots. I turn
the knob but the front door
won't budge. Drifts that deep.
I try the back. Same thing.
The kid in me gets happy.
I shake North awake and announce
we're trapped. North says
nothing. Barefoot in underwear
he goes to the living room
and climbs out a window.

# Good Money

When we stop crunching
over drifts of snow, what sounds
at first like silence gives way
to the immense agony
of the whole frozen lake
shifting, its great sheet of ice
moaning against the limitation
of land. In the shallows, icefishing
tents sit darkly in starlight,
pitched far apart like farms.
Yesterday North told me
he's been offered a permanent job
fishing in Alaska and now
we're drunk and talking
about the past. We walk toward
the middle. Snow and ice
paint patterns on the lake
as stark as the coats of zebras.
Remember, North says, when
I convinced you crab apples
are poisonous? I smile:
Remember that guy who told us
aliens are after earth's gold?
North doubles over, laughing
so hard it makes no noise.

Aliens! He's crying now.
Aliens love gold so much.
We circle more precisely
to the middle, as if seeking
every privacy the lake can afford.
It's good money, he says.
Now we're getting there.
We don't need money.
No, he says, *you* don't need money.
I stop walking. I try to imagine
the North I met ten years ago
talking this way. You can't
keep bailing out your dad,
I say, but even as I say it
I regret it. He takes a swig.
You wanna talk dads?
What about yours—what happens
when you don't have his handouts?
Behind him, cars crawl
the shoreline like Christmas lights
strung around a garage door,
the darkness of his face
like a bad bulb in the pattern.
I grope around for anything
that might convince him.

It's worse than this, I joke.
No, he says, it's actually warmer
where I'm going. The moan
of the lake comes again, low
and vast like outer space
expanding. *Where I'm going.*
Over the houses to the west
a cloud is red, then white,
then red, as a cellphone tower
keeps its steady pulse.

# IV

# Eviction Day

After curbing what hasn't sold
I sit across the street and spy on people
taking what this morning was mine.
A woman and her son struggle
my dresser into a van. A metalhead
straps my mattress to his roof, caution
tape curlicuing as he revs away.
I feel like a director watching
the set of my play get broken
down before the curtain ever opened.
Nobody wants my orchid, my dog-
eared books. A middleschooler
picks up my Nirvana shirt, sniffs
the pits, measures it against his chest.
I close my eyes as he decides.

# The Gift

In every memory you wear the same
threadbare sweater. Hem stained
with huckleberries and Pennzoil.
Elbows worn through, then darned,
then worn through again. Giving way
at both shoulders, the seams
leave stitches loose in midair.
The collar is almost severed—
it hovers above the chest
like a necklace. I can mend it,
you'd said, even the mistakes
in the braided cables, knitted by hand
when you were little more
than a boy. Your mother
wanted it to last, I remember
the story going, so the size
was for a future you,
your final height predicted
by an awkward middle school
stage, late adjustments
based on your father's build.
By the time you and I met,
an unraveling cuff exposed
half your forearm's boat tattoo,
the waistband wouldn't stop

riding up and had to be
pulled forever downward.
Your mother's estimates of you
were modest. Not mine.
In my mind you will always be
hunched over a needle, fixing
what was wrong from the start.

# The Family

In perfect synchrony with the family
rising from the booth and laughing
their way toward the door, I ditch
my coffee on the counter and slide in
where they've been. I wolf the father's
Reuben and move to the daughter's
grilled cheese. I make quick work
of melted milkshakes, no looking up
to see if I'm seen. And although
I'm counting each second it takes to pound
the leftover plates, at the end of it
I wipe my lips with a cloth napkin
and linger, letting myself imagine
a wife and kids gone on a trip
to the bathroom, hot water running
as she scrubs Mrs. Butterworth's
from their fingers, fixes their hair.
The waitress comes for dishes, too involved
in her own life to notice I don't have
the right clothes, the right face.
Yes, I say. We're finished.

# Food Stamps Interview

I don't lie, but I try to make myself
sound worse off than I am. Unemployed?
Yes. Uninsured? Definitely. She wipes
her hands and napkin-pats her lips before
returning to the keyboard, working on
a jelly donut as we go. Any prospects?
No. Any temporary benefits? No.
Do you take medication? Shamelessly
I weigh what's most mysterious.
Undiagnosed, I say, but whatever she types
is much longer than that. She takes
the next bite. Address? None
at the moment. Connections? I ask
what she means. Do you have people?
I hesitate, then make them vanish.

# New Place

Unpacking the last box, I happen on this
picture of him, a stranger I once lived with
month-to-month while I looked for something

cheaper. He lost his arm at seven when
his brother made him climb a telephone pole
and touch the live wire. The fall should've

killed me, he said, but I landed in a garden bed
our neighbor had recently turned. I had to relearn
how to write, how to draw, how to throw a ball.

Late at night we'd talk about our brothers,
how hard it was to forgive. He loved bragging
about the amount he could handle: make a call,

pound a burger, and drive stick shift all at once.
When we juggled clubs he'd tease me for using two
hands but we both knew we needed three

to make the pattern work. I don't know where
he is now, or what he does, or if he's in touch
with his brother. In the photograph he's jammed

himself into the small gap between the mirror
and clawfoot tub. Eyes shut, smirking, he lifts
his palm into the air which perfectly doubles

its reflection so he looks like a priest offering
benediction. I don't remember taking it,
but someone did, and I was the only one there.

# Living Alone

Another day of not seeing
anyone but the faces

on TV. For company
I record my impressions

of celebrities and play
them back, but the voices

don't sound like them
and don't sound like me.

I peel an orange
and smell my hands. I read

portions of a mystery
in different rooms

to make it feel like different
things are happening.

The longer I'm alone
the smaller a gesture could be

and still console
or rattle me. Strange to need

so little, but to need it
so badly. I step into the air

conditioning of Target
and ask after brands

I know they carry
just to hear someone say yes.

# Mushrooming

You pointed at the ground. Where?
I said. There was nothing there—

logs softened from a long season
under snow. Kneeling, you eased

your fingers between rotten leaves
and from nowhere delivered

a fat mushroom to my empty palm.
You pointed again: Nothing.

You could see things I couldn't.
And it would have been human

for you to want to keep it
like that. But instead you armycrawled

the damp showing me how
to read the lumps in the leaves.

Money lumps, we laughed.
Is there a way to get back

to that feeling? I still smile
at our wild guesses: Two hundred

per pound, two-fifty. And later,
after drying and dividing

into ounces, I tallied our take
to the penny, even though

we kept them for ourselves
and ate them all in omelets.

# Dimple

Sadder than believing you're alone
in this world is believing
you're alone while others exist.
Have I let it come to this?
Can it be true the early humans
roamed the earth in tiny clans
and could name in perfect darkness
anyone they loved from nothing
but a whiff of their particular
sweat? I go back to the last
conversation we had. An argument.
And near the end of it, sensing
your voice soften to let me in,
why couldn't I stop my gaze
from faltering and landing
on the dimple of your chin?
It was the smallest change. Or maybe
the smallest refusal to change.
Almost nothing. But enough.

# The Mattress

No car to drive to the dump and too embarrassed
to borrow one, you scrape the black mold
off the underside as best you can, muscle it
onto your shoulder. Spores multiplied to the size
of you, the rough shape, born night after night
by the heat of your sleep. So late you lurch
down Hennepin without notice. Turning
at Taylor you pause between streetlights, crease
the mattress in half and squat on the fold
so you won't have to face it. You're almost
to the bridge when a cop's spotlight throws
the awful bulk of your shadow on concrete.
Where you going with that thing?
You make up a story. Is it yours? You admit it is.
Not your best look, Junior. Yes, you play along,
I should change. The cruiser turns down 8th
and a moment later a coal train rattles under
the bridge on its way out of the country. You brace
the mattress on the guardrail and pivot
the weight, torquing it down through the dark
where it lands on the black coal and pulls
north like shame itself on a conveyer belt,
the mold gazing up at you like the aborted face
of what, all by yourself, you have made.

# Lay It Bare

I know you're hungry for it.
More money. More news. Desperate

for any laurel that parades you
as happier than you know

you are. A car. A cruise. Some haircut
reeking so deeply of depression

no one with a nose could miss it.
Making more each year. Spending

more. The pride of how little
time you have to spare. I know

I embarrass you, still living
on expired food I find, dented tuna

I squirrel away, spending at a pace slower
than a pulse. Slow, that's what

I have. I'm not happy either.
I walk past bars where flush people

drink. Markets where I dumpster
what I eat. Down streets quiet enough

to hush the last ten years. Parks
dark enough to find Gemini, Lyra.

I don't wish you were poor.
I wish you were here.

V

# Contact

*Be careful—I'm filled with glass.*
*Two broken cans inside me.*
*I'm the good stuff, open me first.*
I didn't want to trust the messages,
scrawled in Sharpie on scraps
of cardboard, but sure enough: glass,
the two busted cans, the good stuff.
I'd worked this dumpster
for years, been caught a few times,
but nobody had ever tried
to communicate with me.
*You'll want me,* the next one said.
*How about a little something sweet*
*for the weekend?* One night
I hid as the staff brought out
the trash, but when I couldn't
figure who was helping me,
my need to know got worse.
Business hours I pretended
to shop, spied on the bag boys,
made wild guesses. Meanwhile
elaborate cartoons began to coil
around the messages—a troop
of monkeys meant bananas,

a school of fish meant sushi.
What else could I do? *Thank you,*
I wrote in the branches above
the monkeys. *Thank you,* I wrote
in the ocean below the fins.

NOTES

"Cora" is for Anessa Ibrahim

"Snow" is for Morris Wee

"Lou" is for Olaf Carlson-Wee

"B&B" is for Kristine Carlson

"Trash" is for North Spring

"House Fear" is after Robert Frost's "The Hill Wife" (section II)

"New Place" is for Kai Carlson-Wee

"Mushrooming" is for Nathan Barnard

"Contact" is for whoever you were

## ACKNOWLEDGMENTS

I wish to thank the National Endowment for the Arts, Poets & Writers, the McKnight Foundation, the Camargo Foundation, the Ucross Foundation, the Napa Valley Writers' Conference, and Vanderbilt University, with whose support these poems were written.

Grateful acknowledgment is made to the following publications where these poems first appeared, some in earlier versions:

*32 Poems*: "Barb"
*American Poetry Review*: "Call and Response," "Cups," "Dimple,"
    "House Fear," "Mushrooming"
*Code Lit*: "Another Thrill"

*The Common*: "Moving Sale"
*Harvard Review*: "The Family"
*Los Angeles Review of Books*: "Ambition"
*New England Review*: "Footprint," "The Juggler," "Trash"
*Oxford American*: "Lay It Bare," "Spirits," "Where I'm From"
*The Paris Review*: "Cora," "Hired"
*Prairie Schooner*: "Good Money"
*Rattle*: "Oscar," "Where I'm At"
*Smartish Pace*: "Sea Change"
*Southern Humanities Review*: "Caught"
*The Southern Review*: "The Gift," "Gout," "Listening to North in
    the Morning," "Living Alone," "Snow"
*The Sun*: "I Feel Sorry For Aliens"
*Virginia Quarterly Review*: "B&B," "Contact," "Eviction Day,"
    "Food Stamps Interview," "Lou," "The Mattress," "New Place"

"Hired" and "The Family" were featured on *The Paris
    Review*'s EBSCO Poetry Project

Thanks to Dorianne Laux, B. H. Fairchild, Claudia Emerson, Ada
Limón, Mark Jarman, Kate Daniels, Beth Bachmann, Rick Hilles,
Lorrie Moore, Joan Larkin, A. Van Jordan, Bruce Beasley, Oliver
de la Paz, Stan Tag, Mary Cornish, and Dalen Towne—for your
teaching and mentoring, which have profoundly blessed me.

Thanks to Adrian Matejka, Maggie Smith, Patrick Phillips, and
Luis Alberto Urrea—for your words of support.

Thanks to Dan Haney, Chris Ketchum, Carla Diaz, Grady Chambers, Michael Bazzett, Leslie Bazzett, Gregory Pardlo, Jennifer Grotz, Ross White, Laura Kasischke, Patrick Rosal, Emily Nemens, Jessica Faust, Wes Enzinna, Todd Boss, Elizabeth Scanlon, Major Jackson, Rebecca Gayle Howell, Sam Cheney, Devon Walker-Figueroa, Justin Boening, Matthew Wimberley, Matthew Baker, Jenessa Abrams, Rick Barot, Eduardo C. Corral, Traci Brimhall, Adam Latham, Michael Torres, Max McDonough, Tarfia Faizullah, Jamaal May, Patty Paine, George David Clark, Corey Van Landingham, Chris Kempf, Francine Conley, Kevin Morgan Watson, Michael Kleber-Diggs, Nikki Shaner-Bradford, Kwame Dawes, Timothy Green, Maudelle Driskell, Patrick Donnelly, Stephen Reichert, Eric Lorberer, Maggie Blake Bailey, Joy Priest, Sandee Gertz, Beth Haverkamp Powers, Taylor Brorby, Andrew Snee, Nancy Holochwost, Matt Hart, Christopher P. Locke, Matt Miller, Patrick Halmrast, Nathan Barnard, Bretta Ballou, and Steve Ringo—for your friendship and support.

My deepest thanks to my editor, Jill Bialosky.

My deepest thanks to my agent, Rob McQuilkin.

All my gratitude and love to Edgar Kunz, Scott Lyon, and North Spring.

All my gratitude and love to Anessa Ibrahim.

All my gratitude and love to Mom, Dad, Kai, and Olaf.

ABOUT THE AUTHOR

Anders Carlson-Wee is the author of *The Low Passions*, a New York Public Library Book Group Selection, and *Dynamite*, winner of the Frost Place Chapbook Prize. His work has appeared in *The Paris Review*, *Harvard Review*, *American Poetry Review*, *Buzzfeed*, *Ploughshares*, *Virginia Quarterly Review*, *The Sun*, *The Southern Review*, *The Best American Nonrequired Reading*, and many other publications. The recipient of a fellowship from the National Endowment for the Arts, he is the winner of the Poetry International Prize. His work has been translated into Chinese. Anders holds an MFA from Vanderbilt University and is represented by Massie & McQuilkin Literary Agents. He lives in Los Angeles.

www.anderscarlsonwee.com